AF726954

www.ingramcontent.com/pod-product-compliance
Ingram Content Group UK Ltd.
Pitfield, Milton Keynes, MK11 3LW, UK
UKHW062001290726
14090UKWH00021B/1318

9 781763 602342

I Love Arabic series
Kindergarten (Part two)

Published By:
Arabic Joyride Press

We are proud to announce that this workbook is being distributed to the **Australian Arabic Academy**, supporting their mission to promote Arabic language and culture. Our sincere thanks to the Academy for their partnership and dedication to Arabic education.

Written by:
Widad Salman & Kawthar Joudeh

Illustrated by:
Kawthar Joudeh

ISBN: 978-1-7636023-4-2

سلسلة أنا أحب العربية – المرحلة الابتدائية (الجزء الثاني)

نشر بواسطة

Arabic Joyride Press

نحن فخورون بالإعلان عن أن هذا الكتاب يتم توزيعه من خلال الأكاديمية الأسترالية للغة العربية، دعماً لمهمتهم في تعزيز اللغة والثقافة العربية . نقدم شكرنا الجزيل للأكاديمية على شراكتهم واهتمامهم بتعليم اللغة العربية

تأليف :
وداد سلمان وكوثر جودة

تصميم :
كوثر جودة

ISBN: 978-1-7636023-4-2

I Love Arabic

Parents' and Teachers' Guide

Kindergarten - Part Two

Unlock the joy of learning Arabic with your child or student through this engaging and colourful book! Filled with fun exercises and vibrant illustrations, this book makes learning Arabic an exciting adventure.

What's Inside:
This workbook is part of the 'I Love Arabic - Kindergarten' series, published by Arabic Joyride Press. It is the second part and covers 8 Arabic letters. Each letter is introduced as an individual lesson with a thoughtfully arranged sequence.

Detailed Lessons:
Every lesson covers:

- One letter per lesson (shapes of the letter when joining - Beginning, Middle, and End)
- Friendly and unfriendly letters (a detailed parents' and teachers' guide)
- Heavy and light letters (a detailed parents' and teachers' guide)
- The letter with short vowels
- Colours in Arabic
- Shapes in Arabic
- Arabic vocabulary
- Activities on tracing the letters and numbers

Repetitive Learning:
All alphabet lessons are crafted in a repetitive way, explaining short vowels, heavy and light letters, friendly and unfriendly letters, and the shapes of letters at the beginning, middle, and end. This repetition allows sufficient time for students to absorb the basics and implement them easily and effectively.

Alphabet Guide:
The Arabic alphabet in its original order is included at the start and end of this workbook, allowing students to eventually memorise it as a song or through other methods, complementing the series' unique approach. The authors have chosen a unique sequence rather than the traditional alphabetical order, allowing students to effectively recognise each letter individually without referring to the alphabetical song. Each of the 8 letters is carefully selected and introduced in groups or individually, depending on the similarities in letters' shapes, sounds, and characteristics.

دليل للآباء والمعلمين

افتح باب تعلم اللغة العربية مع طفلك أو تلميذك من خلال هذا الكتاب المليء بالتمارين الممتعة والرسومات الزاهية! يجعل هذا الكتاب تعلم اللغة العربية مغامرة مثيرة.

ما بداخل الكتاب:

هذا الكتاب هو جزء من سلسلة "أحب العربية – المرحلة الابتدائية"، والتي قامت بنشرها شركة Arabic Joyride Press . إنه الجزء الثاني ويغطي ثمانية حروف من اللغة العربية. يتم تقديم كل حرف كدرس فردي بترتيب مدروس

كل درس يشمل الآتي

- حرفًا واحدًا لكل درس (أشكال الحرف عند التوصيل – البداية، الوسط، والنهاية)
- الحروف المتعاونة وغير المتعاونة (دليل مفصل للآباء و المعلمين)
- الحروف المفخمة و المرققة (دليل مفصل للآباء و المعلمين)
- الحرف مع الحركات القصيرة
- المفردات العربية
- أنشطة على ممارسة كتابة الحروف و الأرقام
- الأشكال بالعربية
- الألوان بالعربية

التعلم التكراري
تم تصميم دروس الحروف بطريقة تكرارية، تشرح الحركات القصيرة، الحروف المفخمة و المرققة، الحروف المتعاونة و غير المتعاونة وأشكال الحروف في البداية و الوسط والنهاية. هذا التكرار يسمح للطلاب باستوعاب أساسيات اللغة العربية وتنفيذها بسهولة وفعالية

دليل الحروف الأبجدية
تشمل الحروف الأبجدية العربية بترتيبها الأصلي في بداية ونهاية هذا الكتاب، مما يسمح للطلاب في النهاية بحفظها كأغنية أو من خلال طرق أخرى، مكملة نهج السلسلة الفريد. اختار المؤلفون ترتيبًا فريدًا بدلاً من الترتيب الأبجدي التقليدي، مما يسمح للطلاب بالتعرف على كل حرف بشكل فعال دون الرجوع إلى الأغنية الأبجدية. تم اختيار كل من الحروف بعناية وتقديمها في مجموعات أو بشكل فردي، اعتمادًا على تشابهات أشكال وأصوات وخصائص الحروف

I Love Arabic

Kindergarten - Part Two

Why This Book?

- **Quick and Easy Learning:** Designed to help your child or student recognise the Arabic alphabet with short and long vowels quickly.
- **Fun and Interactive:** Every lesson is structured to be enjoyable and easy to understand.
- **Versatile Use:** Perfect for home learning and school settings. Each lesson includes a homework page for reinforced learning.

Give your child or student a head start in Arabic with this carefully crafted guide that makes learning Arabic a delightful experience!

Important Notes to Consider

Introduction of Letters

In this book series, when explaining each letter, the letters are introduced as they are pronounced with the short vowel Fat-hah and not by their original names.The authors believe this method is better for children at this age to start learning the sound of each letter before learning its name. This approach helps them read words more accurately.

Reference to Original Names:

All alphabets' original names are introduced in order at the beginning of this book for reference.

Special Note on Letters Pronunciation:

It is important to note that the letters ص (<u>S</u>a) and ض (<u>Dh</u>a), which are part of the lessons mentioned in this workbook, are both heavy letters and do not resemble any letter in English in terms of the exact pronunciation.

To indicate this distinction:

- A line is placed under the letters.

لماذا هذا الكتاب ؟

تعلم سريع وسهل: مصمم لمساعدة طفلك أو طالبك على التعرف على الحروف الأبجدية العربية مع الحركات القصيرة والمدود بسرعة

مرح وتفاعلي: كل درس مصمم ليكون ممتعًا وسهل الفهم

استخدام متعدد: مثالي للتعلم في المنزل والمدارس. كل درس يتضمن صفحة للواجبات لتعزيز التعلم

امنح طفلك أو طالبك بداية قوية في اللغة العربية مع هذا الدليل المصمم بعناية والذي يجعل تعلم اللغة العربية تجربة ممتعة!

ملاحظات هامة يجب مراعاتها

تقديم الحروف

في هذه السلسلة من الكتب، يتم تقديم الحروف عند شرح كل حرف كما يُنطق بالحركة القصيرة الفتحة وليس بأسمائها الأصلية. يعتقد المؤلفون أن هذه الطريقة أفضل للأطفال في هذا العمر ليبدأوا بتعلم صوت كل حرف قبل تعلم اسمه. هذه الطريقة تساعدهم على قراءة الكلمات بدقة أكبر

الإشارة إلى الأسماء الأصلية للحروف الأبجدية

تُعرض أسماء الحروف الأبجدية الأصلية بالترتيب في بداية هذا الكتاب كمرجع

ملاحظة خاصة حول نطق الحروف

من المهم ملاحظة أن الحرفين ص و ض، اللذان هما جزء من الدروس المذكورة في هذا الكتاب، لا يشبهان أي حرف في اللغة الإنجليزية من حيث النطق حيث هما من الحروف المفخمة

للإشارة إلى هذا الفرق، عند كتابتهما باللغة الانجليزية:

تم وضع خط تحتهما <u>S</u>a, <u>Dh</u>a

A Message From The Author

بسم الله الرحمن الرحيم

What inspired me to embark on the journey of writing and publishing this Arabic workbook series is my deep and enduring connection with the Arabic language, cultivated since my teenage years in Kuwait. Immersing myself in this rich language and its endless nuances deepened my love for the Quran. I began sharing this knowledge with my family and those around me, following the teachings of the Prophet Muhammad (PBUH). As my children grew and started families of their own, I taught my grandchildren the importance of preserving their mother tongue, the sacred language of the Quran, recognising that translations can never fully capture the essence of Allah's words.

Over the years, I witnessed firsthand how Muslims in the West struggled with maintaining their connection to the Arabic language, which often compromised their spiritual engagement with the Quran. In my opinion, this is largely due to the inadequacies of existing curricula in Arabic institutions in Australia. These programmes either underestimated students' capacity to learn Arabic quickly or overwhelmed them with overseas syllabi that were not tailored to the needs of bilingual students from non-native Arabic backgrounds.

This workbook series is designed to bridge that gap. It provides a comprehensive and practical approach to learning Arabic, guiding students from basic dialects to Arabic Fus-ha, enabling them to read and understand the Quran fluently. Importantly, this series is inclusive, catering to students of all linguistic and religious backgrounds. I am honoured to support students worldwide in beginning their Arabic language journey.

May Allah SWT bless my sincere efforts and accept this work as Sadaqah Jariyah for my parents, my husband and his parents, my children, my students, and the broader Muslim community. Ameen.

Sincerely,

Widad Salman

رسالة من المؤلفة

بسم الله الرحمن الرحيم

ما ألهمني لبدء رحلة كتابة ونشر هذه السلسلة من الكتب هو اتصالي العميق والدائم باللغة العربية الذي تم تطويره منذ سنوات مراهقتي في الكويت. غمرت نفسي في هذه اللغة الغنية وتفاصيلها التي لا تنتهي مما عمق حبي للقرآن الكريم. بدأت بمشاركة هذه المعرفة مع عائلتي ومن حولي، متبعةً تعاليم النبي محمد (صلى الله عليه وسلم). عندما كبر أطفالي وبدأوا في تكوين أسرهم الخاصة، علمت أحفادي أهمية الحفاظ على لغتهم الأم، لغة القرآن المقدسة، مدركةً أن الترجمات لا يمكن أن تنقل جوهر كلام الله بشكل كامل.

على مر السنين، شهدت بنفسي كيف كافح المسلمون في الغرب للحفاظ على اتصالهم باللغة العربية، مما أثر غالبًا على ارتباطهم الروحي بالقرآن. في رأيي، يعود ذلك بشكل كبير إلى القصور في المناهج الحالية في المؤسسات العربية و تحديدا في أستراليا كوني أعيش فيها. فإما أن تقلل هذه البرامج من قدرة الطلاب على تعلم اللغة العربية بسرعة، أو تطغى عليهم بالمناهج الخارجية التي لم تكن مصممة لتلبية احتياجات الطلاب ثنائيي اللغة من خلفيات غير ناطقة بالعربية.

تم تصميم سلسلة كتب النشاط هذه لسد تلك الفجوة. فهي توفر نهجًا شاملاً وعمليًا لتعلم اللغة العربية، مما يوفر للطلاب تعلم أساسيات اللغة العربية أولا و من ثم انتقالهم لتعلم اللغة العربية الفصحى بشكل فعال، مما يمكنهم من قراءة القرآن وفهمه بطلاقة. الأهم من ذلك، أن هذه السلسلة شاملة، وتلبي احتياجات الطلاب من جميع الخلفيات اللغوية والدينية. يشرفني دعم الطلاب في جميع أنحاء العالم في بدء رحلتهم في تعلم اللغة العربية.

أسأل الله سبحانه وتعالى أن يبارك في جهودي المخلصة ويتقبل هذا العمل كصدقة جارية لوالدي وزوجي ووالديه وأطفالي وطلابي والمجتمع المسلم الأوسع. آمين.

المخلصة

وداد سلمان

Student information

My name : ....

إِسْمِي : ....

My teacher : ....

مُعَلِّمَتِي : ....

The Alphabet

Thaa' ث	Taa' ت	Baa' ب	Alif أ
Daal د	Khaa' خ	H̄aa' ح	Jeem ج
Seen س	Zaay ز	Raa' ر	Thaal ذ
Taa' ط	Dhaad ض	Saad ص	Sheen ش
Faa' ف	Ghayn غ	Āyn ع	Thaa' ظ
Meem م	Laam ل	Kaaf ك	Qaaf ق
Yaa' ي	Waaw و	Haa' هـ	Noon ن

Nahool and Nahlah are back!

Assalamu Alaikum....

I'ts me again! Nahool!
You might know me from part 1 of the workbook!
I'm happy to be back in this workbook to take you on another fun journey with 8 more Arabic letters!

Assalamu Alaikum....

It's Nahlah!
Open the next page to meet the first letter in this workbook!

Lesson 9 : س Sa

Fish

We are sisters !

س ش

سَمَكَة Samakah

Remember

س Is a light and a friendly letter

أ ب ت ث ج ح خ د ذ ر ز س ش ص ض ط ظ ع غ ف ق ك ل م ن هـ و ي

Trace letter Sa س خَطِّطْ الحَرْفْ

*Start writing from the right

Colour letter س at the beginning of each word aħmar.

سَيَّارَة

سِلْسَالْ

Parets'/Teachers' guide to explaining friendly letters

Friendly letters are letters that can join other letters from both sides (back and front)!

They join by holding hands!

There are 22 friendly letters:

ب ت ث ج ح خ س ش ص ض ط ظ ع غ ف ق ك ل م ن ه و ي

The Letter س is a friendly letter. Look how it holds hands from both sides when joining in the middle of a word:

Now look how the letter س gives only one hand from the front when it joins at the beginning of a word:

And finally, look how the letter س gives only one hand from the back when joining at the end of a word:

Parets'/Teachers' guide to explaining light and heavy letters

There are two types of letters based on pronunciation: (Heavy letters and Light letters).

Heavy letters are letters that are pronouced more heavily and they require more effort to pronounce compared to light letters!

There are Seven Heavy letters:

خ - ص - ض - غ - ط - ق - ظ

The rest of the letters are light:

أ-ب-ت-ث-ج-ح-د-ذ-ر-ز-س-ش-ع-ف-ل-م-ن-ه-ي-و-ك

Heavy letters:

Light letters:

The shapes of Sa س when joining

Letter Sa can change dresses when joining other letters at the:

End — Middle — Beginning

Color letter Sa dresses :
at the beginning aḥmar, in the middle aṣfar and at the end azraq.

سَمَاء — خَسْ — مَسْجِدْ

Introducing short vowels with letter Sa س

There are four short vowels. They are called (Ḥarakaat) (حَرَكَاتْ)

They are symbols (َ ُ ْ ِ) that can sit on top or under letters. (َ) is called Fat-hah, (ُ) is called Dammah and (ْ) is called Sukoon.

Fat-hah , Dammah and Sukoon can sit only on top of letters.

Imagine them as hats! 

(ِ) is called Kasrah, it can sit only under letters.

Imagine Kasrah as a sock! 

With Fat-ḥah Sa س

With Dammah Su س

With Sukoon/Silent S س

With Kasrah Si س

Match letter Sa س with its suitable hat or sock.

سَ سُ سْ سِ

Trace letter Sa with short vowels.

Match letter Sa with the correct word.

جَرَسْ

Bell Jaras

سُلْحُفَاة

Turtle Sulhufaah

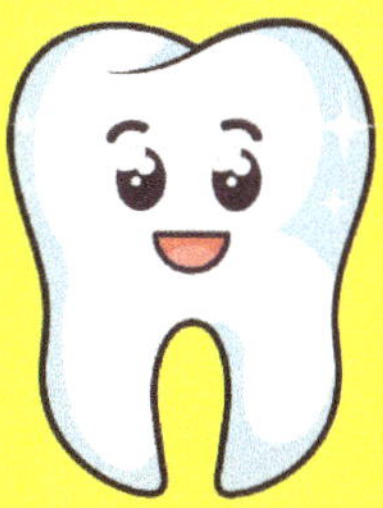

سِنْ

Tooth Sin

سَجَدَ

He prostrated Sajada

س

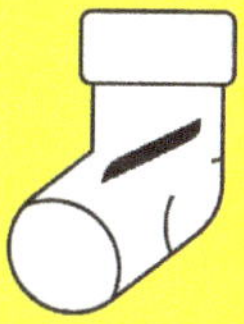

س

س

س

Trace letter Sa س at the beginning, middle and end.

The shapes in Arabic-Revision

Color all (mustateel)s akhdar, (murabaā)s zahry, (daa'irah)s asfar and (muthallath)s burtuqaaly.

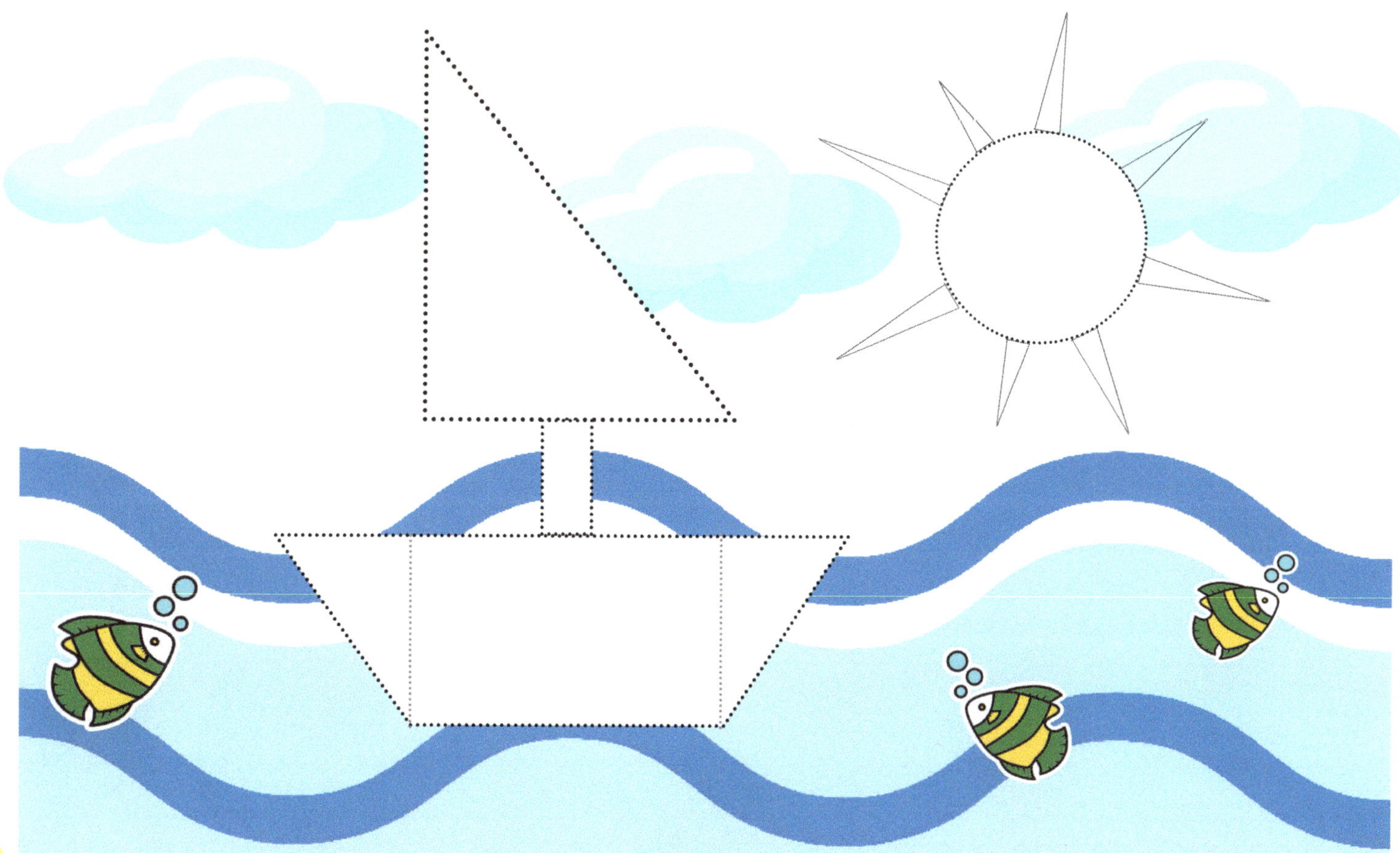

The Arabic numbers

Fourteen-Arbaāata Āashar

أَرْبَعَةَ عَشَرْ

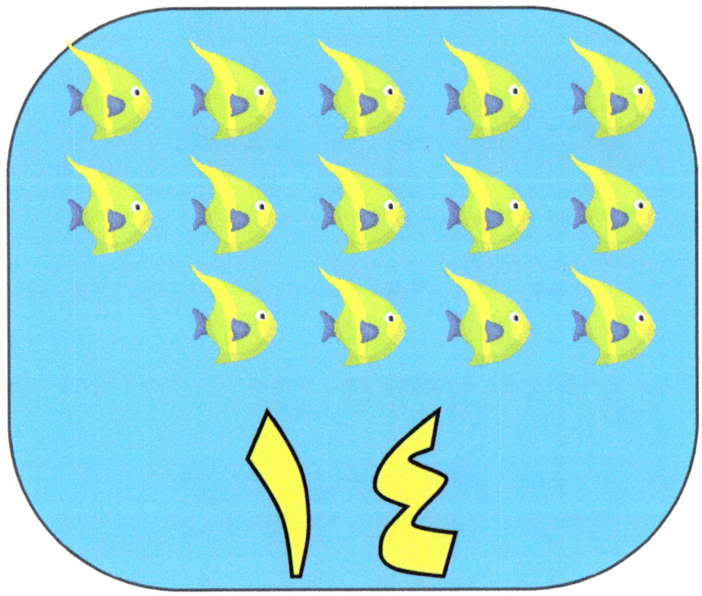

Fifteen-Khamsata Āashar

خَمْسَةَ عَشَرْ

Trace.

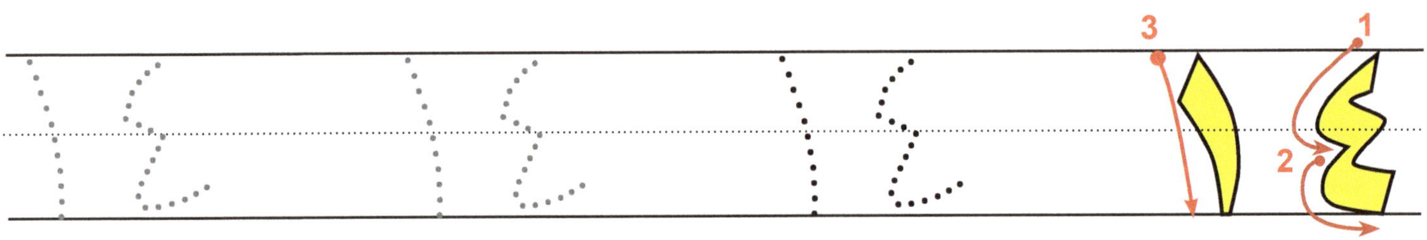

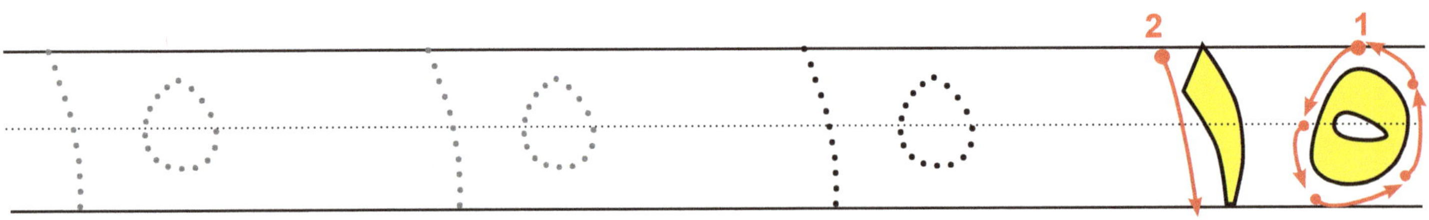

Revision

How many turtles (Sulh̄ufaah)s can you see in each picture?

Write the Arabic number in the ah̄mar أَحْمَر daa'irah.

Trace.

Lets write our homework !

Copy letter Sa س inside the dresses.

Beginning

Middle

End

Lets write our homework !

Copy the numbers.

١٤

١٥

Color the sudaacy akhdar and the rest of the shapes abyadh.

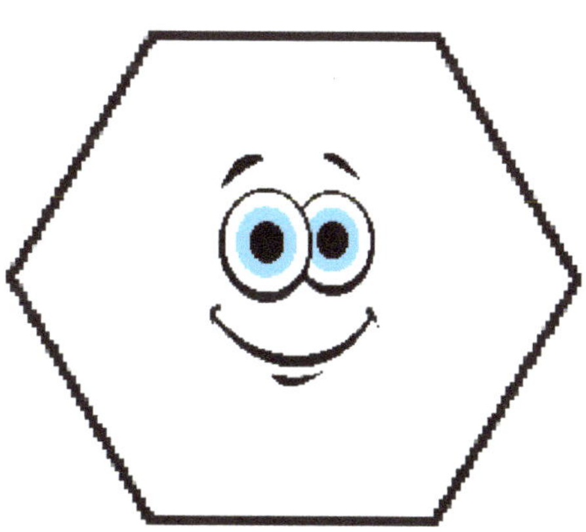

Lesson 10 : ش Sha

Sun

شَمْسْ Shams

Remember

ش Is a light and a friendly letter

أ ب ت ث ج ح خ د ذ ر ز س ش ص ض ط ظ ع غ ف ق ك ل م ن هـ و ي

Trace letter Sha ش خَطِّطْ الحَرْف

*Start writing from the right

Colour letter ش at the beginning of each word zahry.

شَجَرَة

شَوْكَة

ش Is a friendly letter

Look how it holds hands from both sides when joining in the middle of a word:

Now look how the letter ش gives only one hand from the front when it joins at the beginning of a word:

And finally, look how the letter ش gives only one hand from the back when joining at the end of a word:

أ ب ت ث ج ح خ د ذ ر ز س ش ص ض ط ظ ع غ ف ق ك ل م ن هـ و ي

The shapes of Sha ش when joining

Letter Sha can change dresses when joining other letters at the:

End	Middle	Beginning

Color letter Sha dresses :
at the beginning banafsajy, in the middle azraq and at the end bonny.

عَرْشْ شَعْرْ مِنْشَارْ

letter Sha ش with short vowels

With Fat-ħah	Sha		شَ
With Dammah	Shu		شُ
With Sukoon/Silent	Sh		شْ
With Kasrah	Shi		شِ

Match letter Sha ش with its suitable hat or sock.

شُ شِ شَ شْ

Trace letter Sha with short vowels.

Match letter Sha with the correct word.

شِرَاعْ

Sail Shiraaā

شَمْعَة

Candle Shamāah

عَرْشْ

Throne Āarsh

شُعْلَة

Flame Shuālah

ش

ش
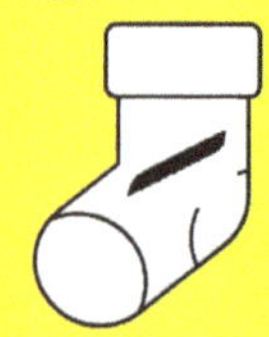

ش

ش

Trace letter Sha ش at the beginning, middle and end.

The shapes in Arabic-Revision

Color all (sudaasy)s burtuqaaly, (Mustateel)s akhdar, (daa'irah)s ahmar and (qalb)s zahry.

The Arabic numbers

Sixteen-Sittata Āashar

سِتَّةَ عَشَرْ

Seventeen-Sabāata Āashar

سَبْعَةَ عَشَرْ

Trace.

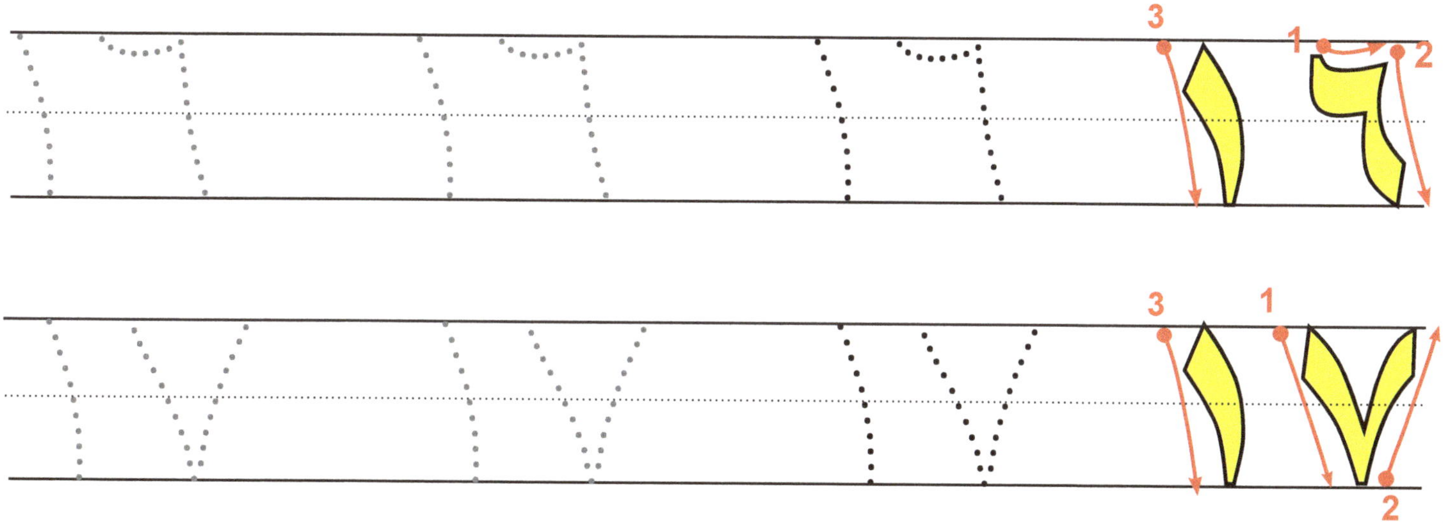

Revision

How many stars (najmah)s can you see in each picture?

Write the Arabic number in the zahry زَهْرِي qalb.

Trace.

أ ب ت ث ج ح خ د ذ ر ز س ش ص ض ط ظ ع غ ف ق ك ل م ن هـ و ي

Lets write our homework !

Copy letter Sha ش inside the dresses.

Beginning

Middle

End

Lets write our homework !

Copy the numbers.

3 1 2 ١٦

3 1 2 ١٧

Draw the shape daa'irah then color it bonny.

Lesson 11 : ص Sa

Chick

We are sisters !

ص ض

صُوصْ Sous

Remember

ص Is a heavy and a friendly letter

Trace letter Sa خَطِّطْ الحَرْفْ ص

*Start writing from the right

Colour letter ص at the beginning of each word akhdhar.

صَارُوخْ 

صُنْدُوقْ 

ص Is a friendly letter

Look how it holds hands from both sides when joining in the middle of a word:

Now look how the letter ص gives only one hand from the front when it joins at the beginning of a word:

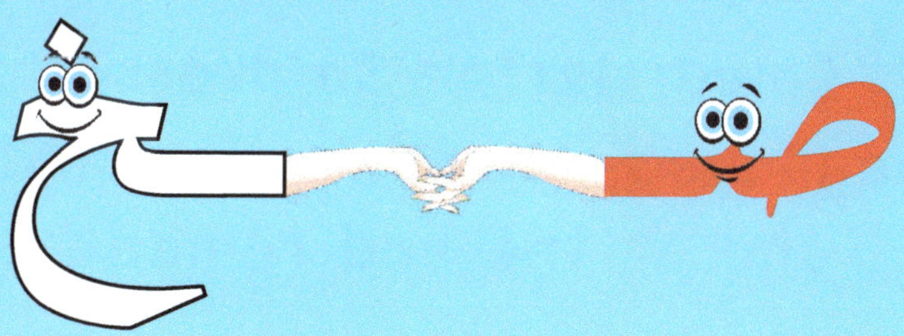

And finally, look how the letter ص gives only one hand from the back when joining at the end of a word:

The shapes of S̲a ص when joining

Letter S̲a can change dresses when joining other letters at the:

End	Middle	Beginning

Colour letter S̲a dresses :
at the beginning **aswad**, in the middle ahmar and at the end ramaady.

بَصَلْ

صَبَّار

مَقَصْ

letter Sa ص with short vowels

With Fat-hah Sa صَ

With Dammah Su صُ

With Sukoon/Silent S صْ

With Kasrah Si صِ

Match letter S̲a ص with its suitable hat or sock.

صْ صِ صُ صَ

Trace letter S̲a with short vowels.

Match letter Sa with the correct word.

صُنْبُور

Tap Sunboor

قَفَصْ

Cage Qafas

صِينِيَّة

Tray Seeniyyah

صَيَّادْ

Fisherman Sayyaad

ص

ص

ص

ص

Trace letter Sa ص at the beginning, middle and end.

ـص ـصـ صـ

ـص ـصـ صـ

ـص ـصـ صـ

ـص ـصـ صـ

ـص ـصـ صـ

The shapes in Arabic-Revision

Trace then colour all (muthallath)s burtuqaaly, (daa'irah)s asfar and (Mustateel)s bonny.

The Arabic numbers

Eighteen-Thamaaniyata Āashar

ثَمَانِيَةَ عَشَرْ

Nineteen-Tisāata Āashar

تِسْعَةَ عَشَرْ

Trace.

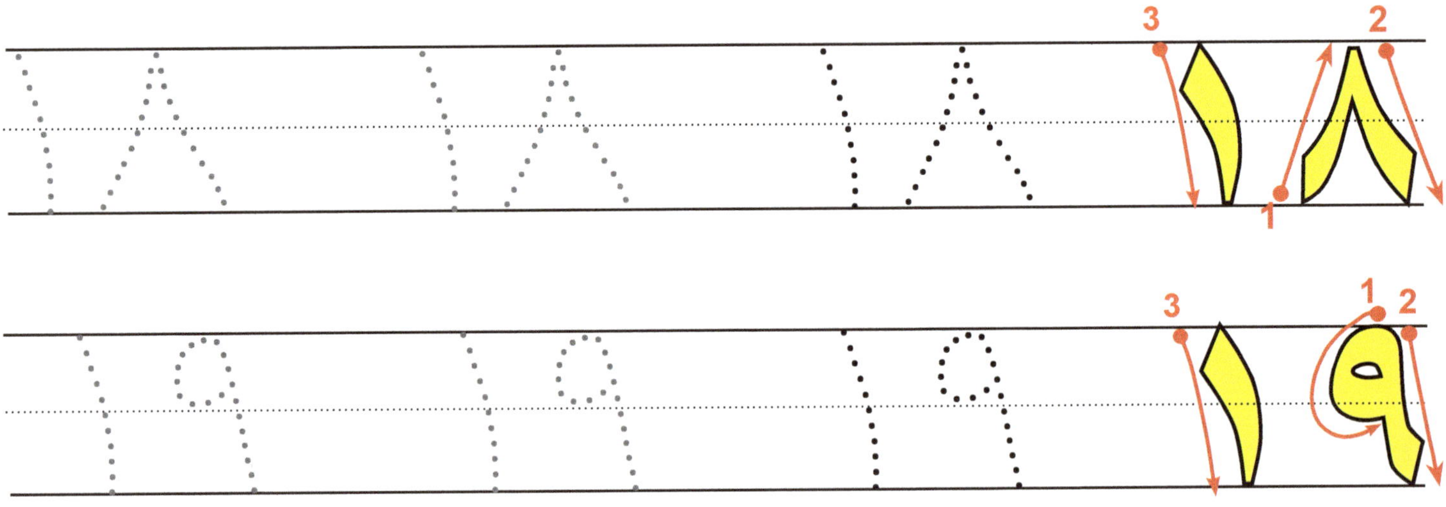

Revision

How many monkeys (qird)s can you see in each picture?

Write the Arabic number in the sudaacy.

Trace.

أ ب ت ث ج ح خ د ذ ر ز س ش ص ض ط ظ ع غ ف ق ك ل م ن هـ و ي

Lets write our homework !

Copy letter S̲a ص inside the dresses.

Beginning

Middle

End

Lets write our homework !

Copy the numbers.

١٨

١٩

Draw the shape muthallath then colour it azraq.

Lesson 12 : ض Dha

Frog

ضِفْدَعْ Dhifdaā

Remember

ض Is a heavy and a friendly letter

أ ب ت ث ج ح خ د ذ ر ز س ش ص ض ط ظ ع غ ف ق ك ل م ن هـ و ي

Trace letter Dha ض خَطِّطْ الحَرْفَ

*Start writing from the right

ض ض ض ض

ض ض ض ض

ض ض ض ض

Colour letter ض at the beginning of each word **banafsajy**.

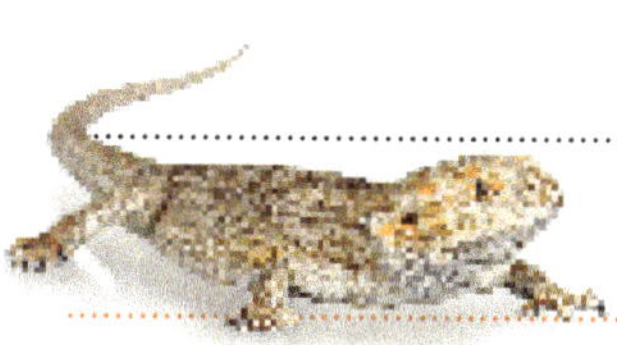

ضَبْ

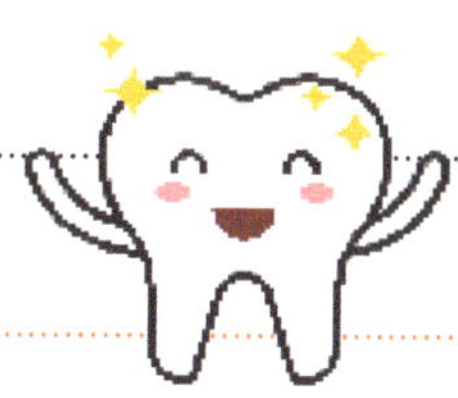

ضِرْسْ

ض Is a friendly letter

Look how it holds hands from both sides when joining in the middle of a word:

Now look how the letter ض gives only one hand from the front when it joins at the beginning of a word:

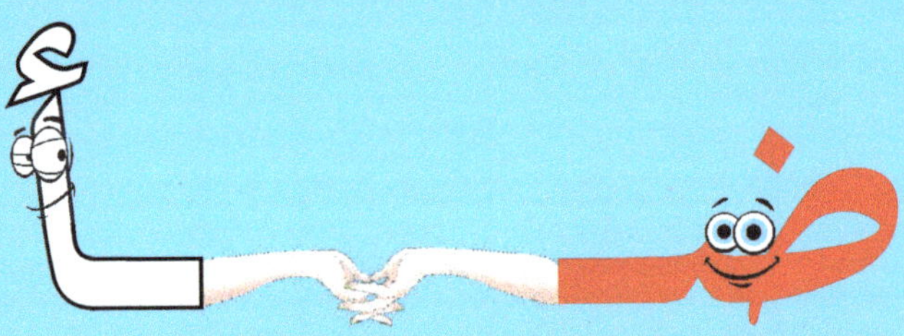

And finally, look how the letter ض gives only one hand from the back when joining at the end of a word:

The shapes of Dha ض when joining

Letter Dha can change dresses when joining other letters at the:

End	Middle	Beginning

Colour letter Dha dresses :
at the beginning abyadh, in the middle **banafsajy** and at the end **aswad**.

ضِرْس مِضْرَب بَيْضْ

With Fat-hah **Dha** ضَ

With Dammah **Dhu** ضُ

With Sukoon/Silent **Dh** ضْ

With Kasrah **Dhi** ضِ

Match letter Dha ضَ with its suitable hat or sock.

ضُ ضِ ضْ ضَ

Trace letter Dha with short vowels.

Match letter Dha with the correct word.

ضَبَابْ

Fog Dhabaab

ضِرْسْ

Molar Dhirs

ضُيُوفْ

Guests Dhuyoof

بَيْضْ

Eggs Baydh

ض

ض

ض

ض

Trace letter Dha ض at the beginning, middle and end.

The shapes in Arabic-Revision

Trace the shapes then colour all (muthallath)s burtuqaaly, (daa'irah)s abyadh, (murabaā)s azraq and (mustateel)s bonny.

The Arabic numbers

Twenty-Īshroon

عِشْرُونْ

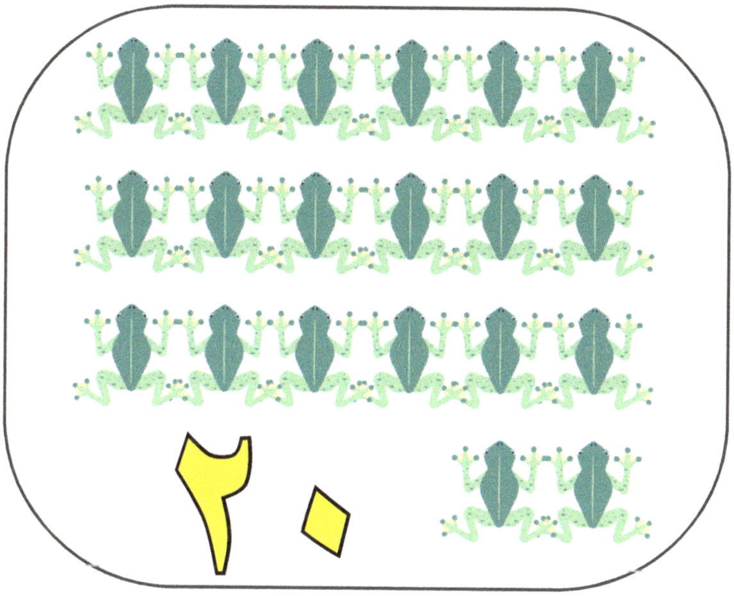

Twenty one-Waahid wa īshroon

وَاحِدْ وَ عِشْرُونْ

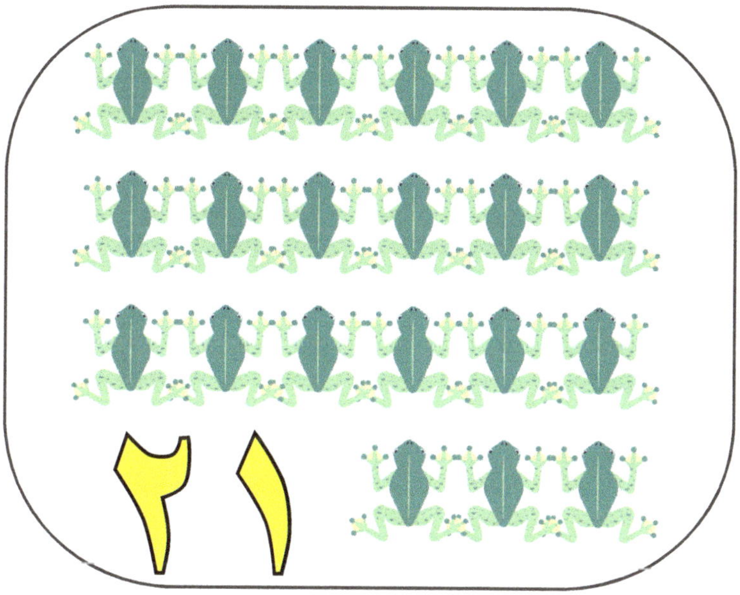

Trace.

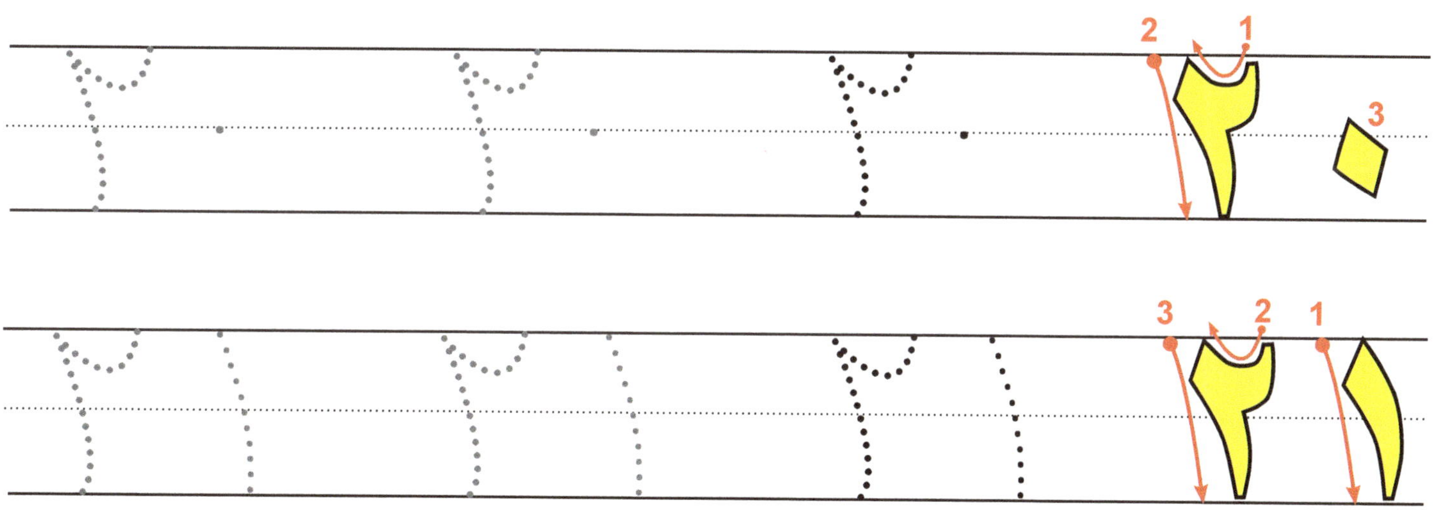

Revision

How many butterflies (faraashah)s can you see in each picture? Write the Arabic number in the murabaā.

Trace.

Lets write our homework !

Copy letter Dha ض inside the dresses.

Beginning

Middle

End

Lets write our homework !

Copy the numbers.

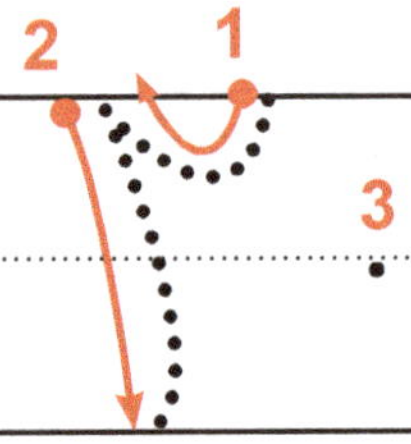

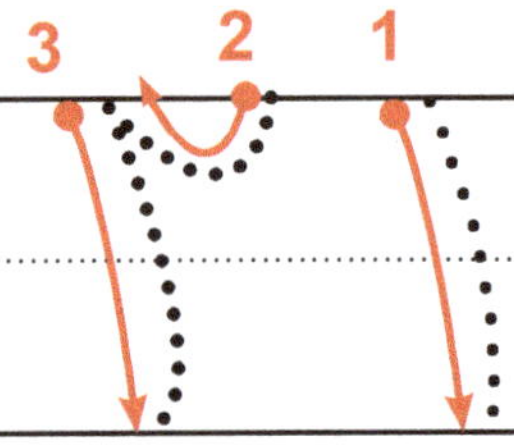

Draw the shape sudaacy then colour it aswad.

Lesson 13 : د Da

Dolphin

We are sisters !

1

د ذ

دُلْفِينْ Dolpheen

Remember

د Is a light and an unfriendly letter!

Trace letter Da د خَطِّطْ الحَرْفْ

*Start writing from the right

1

Colour letter د at the beginning of each word asfar.

 دَرَّاجَة

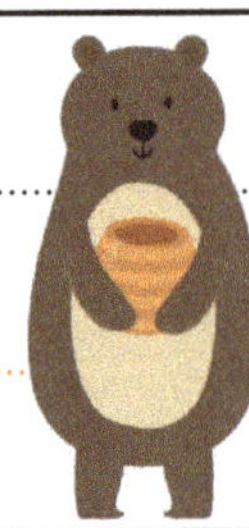 دُبْ

Parets'/Teachers' guide to explaining unfriendly letters

Unfriendly letters are letters that can join other letters only from the back. They join by holdin hands.

There are seven unfriendly letters:

أ ا و د ذ ر ز

Letter د is an unfriendly letter, look how it only holds one hand from the back when joining in the middle of a word:

Parets'/Teachers' guide to explaining unfriendly letters

Now look how letter د is not holding hands from the front when it comes at the beginning of a word:

And finally, look how letter د gives only one hand from the back when joining at the end of a word:

The shapes of Da د when joining

Letter Da can change dresses when joining other letters at the:

Colour letter Da dresses :
at the beginning aḥmar, in the middle banafsajy and at the end azraq.

هَدِيَّة دَفْتَرْ أَسَدْ

With Fat-ḥah	Da	دَ
With Dammah	Du	دُ
With Sukoon/Silent	D	دْ
With Kasrah	Di	دِ

Match letter Da د with its suitable hat or sock.

دُ دَ دْ دِ

Trace letter Da with short vowels.

Match letter Da with the correct word.

دُرَّاقْ

Peach Durraaq

دَجَاجَة

Chicken Dajaajah

وَرْدْ

Flowers Ward

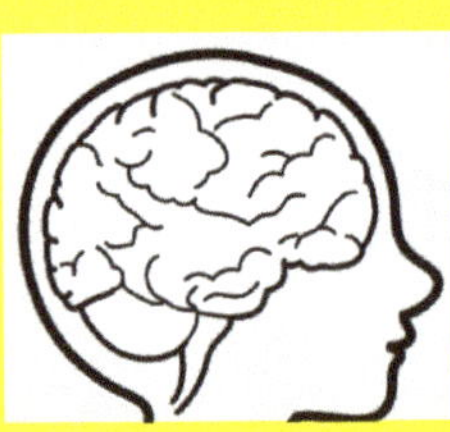

دِمَاغْ

Brain Dimaagh

د

د

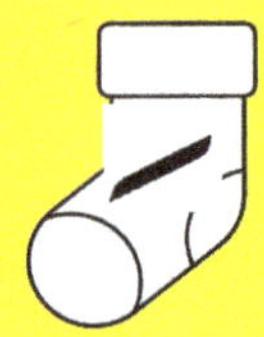

د

د

Trace letter Da د at the beginning, middle and end.

The shapes in Arabic-Revision

Colour all (mustateel)s bonny, (daa'irah)s akhdar, (murabaā)s aswad and (sudaacy)s zahry.

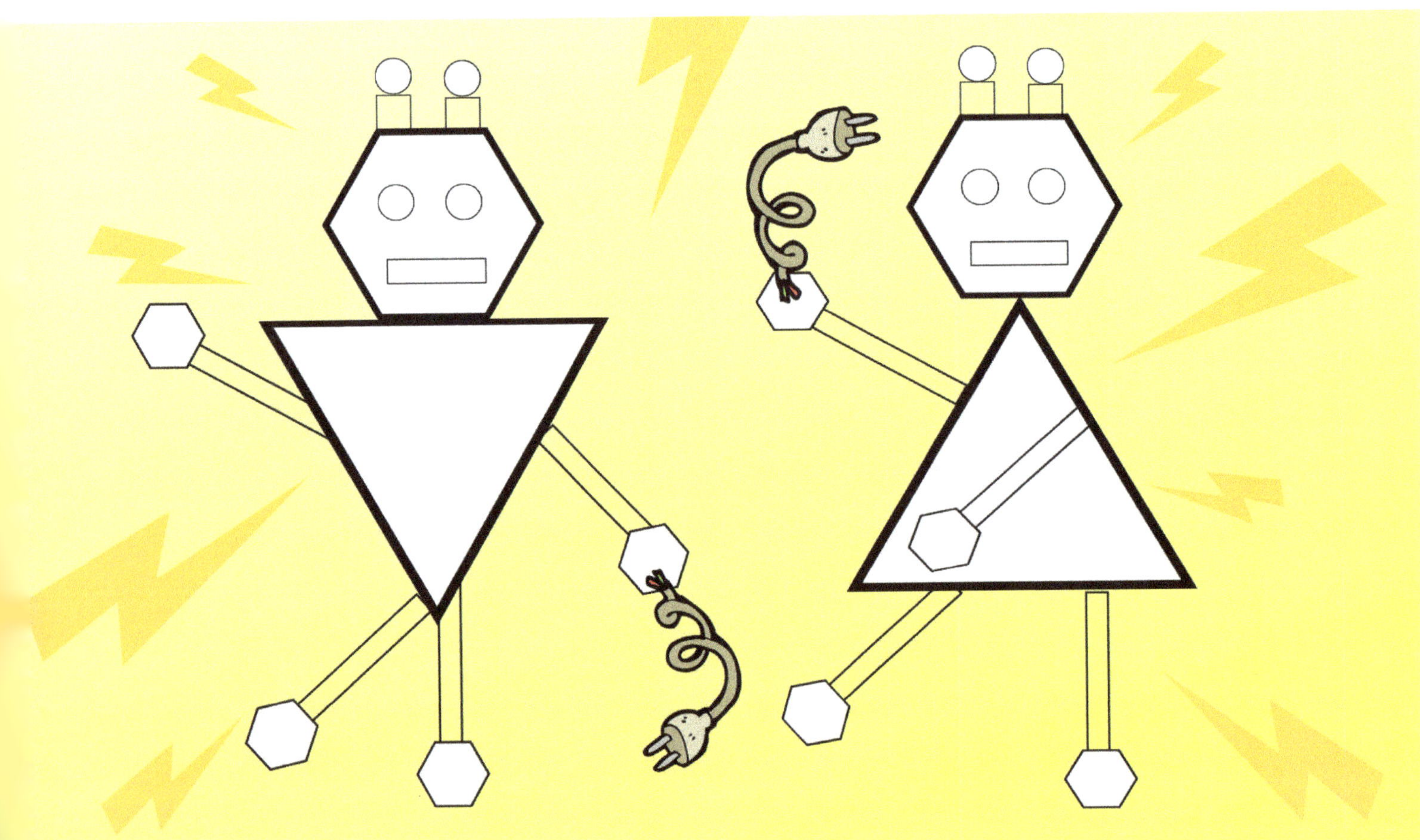

The Arabic numbers

Twenty two-Ithnaan wa īshroon

إِثْنَانْ وَ عِشْرُونْ

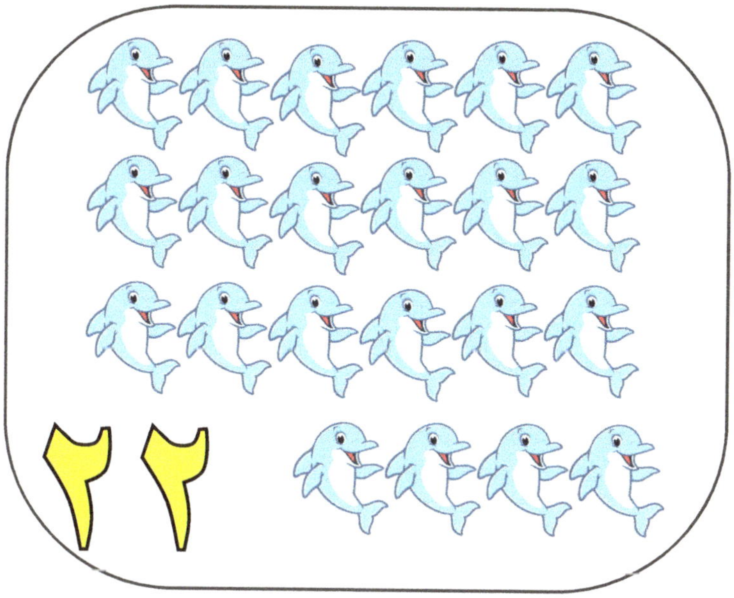

Twenty three-Thalaathah wa īshroon

ثَلَاثَة وَ عِشْرُونْ

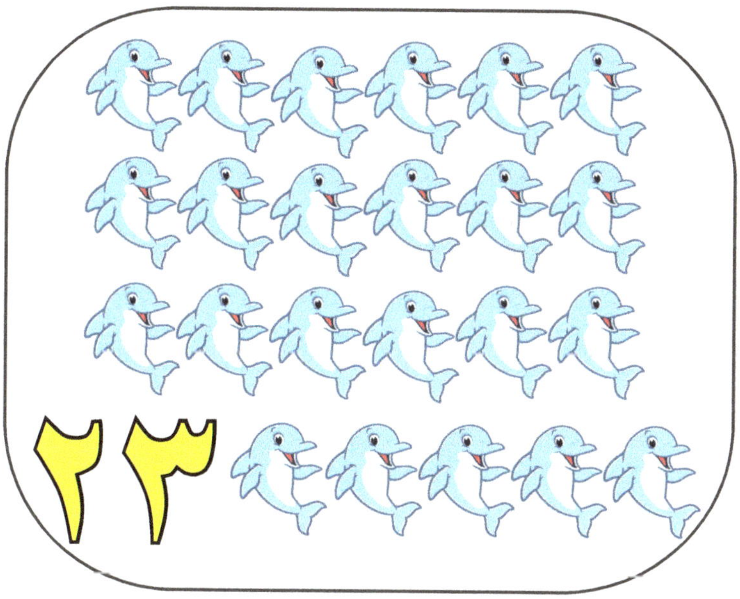

Trace.

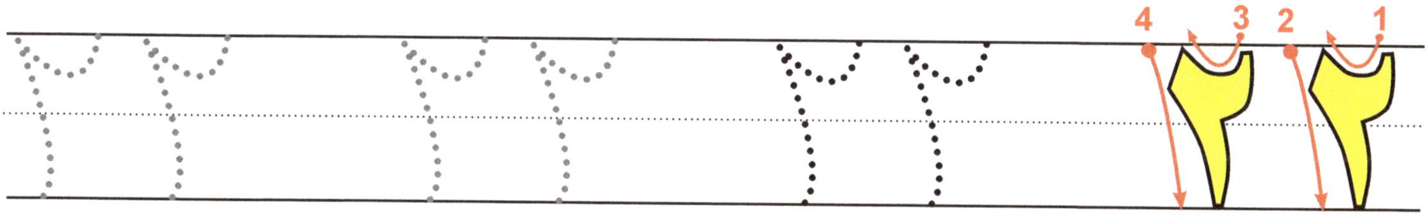

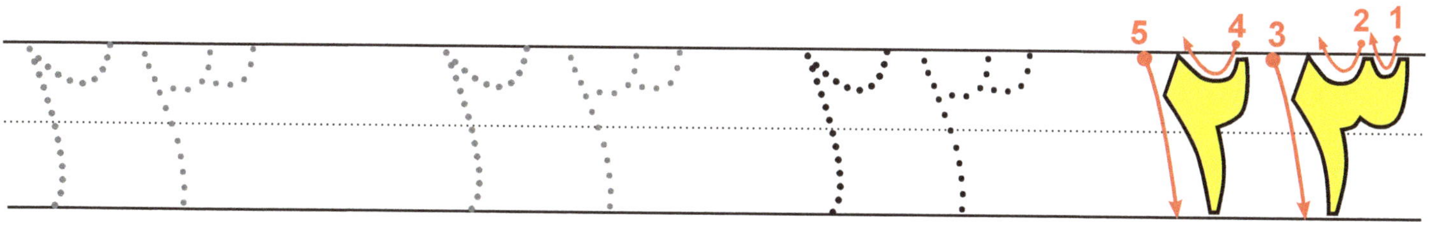

Revision

How many bicycles (darraajah)s can you see in each picture? Write the Arabic number in the qalb.

Trace.

Lets write our homework !

Copy letter Da د inside the dresses.

Beginning

Middle

End

Lets write our homework !

Copy the numbers.

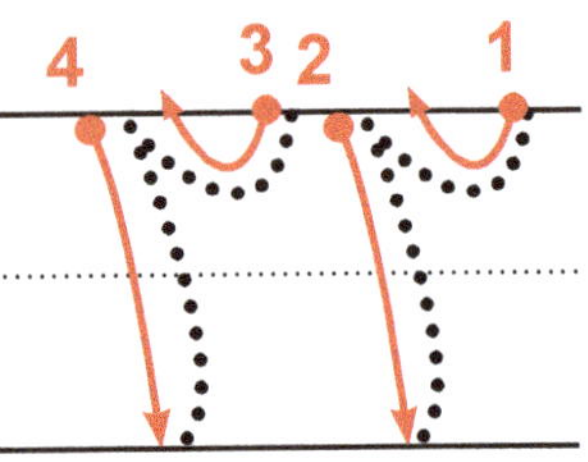

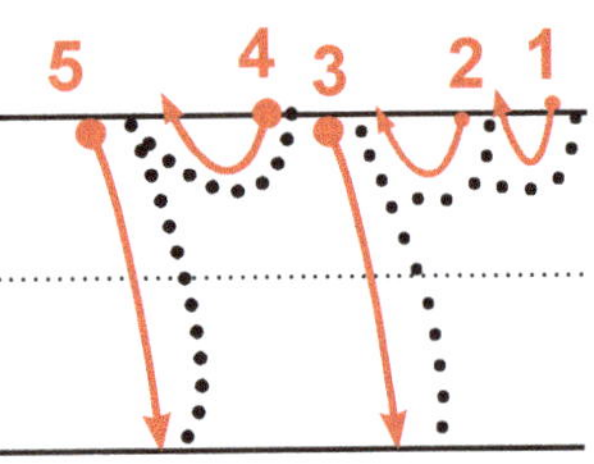

Draw the shape qalb then colour it zahry.

Lesson 14 : ذ Tha

Wolf

We are sisters !

ذِئْبْ Thi’b

Remember

ذ Is a light and an unfriendly letter!

Trace letter Tha ذ خَطِّطْ الحَرْف

*Start writing from the right

ذ ذ ذ ذ

ذ ذ ذ ذ

ذ ذ ذ ذ

Colour letter ذ at the beginning of each word akhdar.

ذُرَة

ذَقْن

ذ Is an unfriendly letter

Letter ذ is an unfriendly letter, look how it only holds one hand from the back when joining in the middle of a word:

Now look how letter ذ is not holding hands from the front when it comes at the beginning of a word:

And finally, look how letter ذ gives only one hand from the back when joining at the end of a word:

The shapes of Tha ذ when joining

Letter Tha can change dresses when joining other letters at the:

End	Middle	Beginning

Colour letter Tha dresses :
at the beginning akhdar, in the middle bonny and at the end burtuqaaly.

ذُبَابْ فَخْذْ نَافِذَة

letter Tha ذ with short vowels

With Fat-ħah | Tha | ذ

With Dammah | Thu | ذ

With Sukoon/Silent | Th | ذ

With Kasrah | Thi | ذ

Match letter Tha ذ with its suitable hat or sock.

ذُ ذِ ذَ ذْ

Trace letter Tha with short vowels.

Match letter Tha with the correct word.

ذِرَاعْ

Arm Thiraaā

ذُبَابَة

Fly Thubaabah

جِذْر

Root Jithr

ذَيْل

Tail Thayl

ذ

ذ

ذ

ذ

Trace letter Tha ذ at the beginning, middle and end.

The Arabic numbers

Twenty four-Arbaāah wa īshroon

أَرْبَعَة وَ عِشْرُونْ

Twenty five-Khamsah wa īshroon

خَمْسَة وَ عِشْرُونْ

Trace.

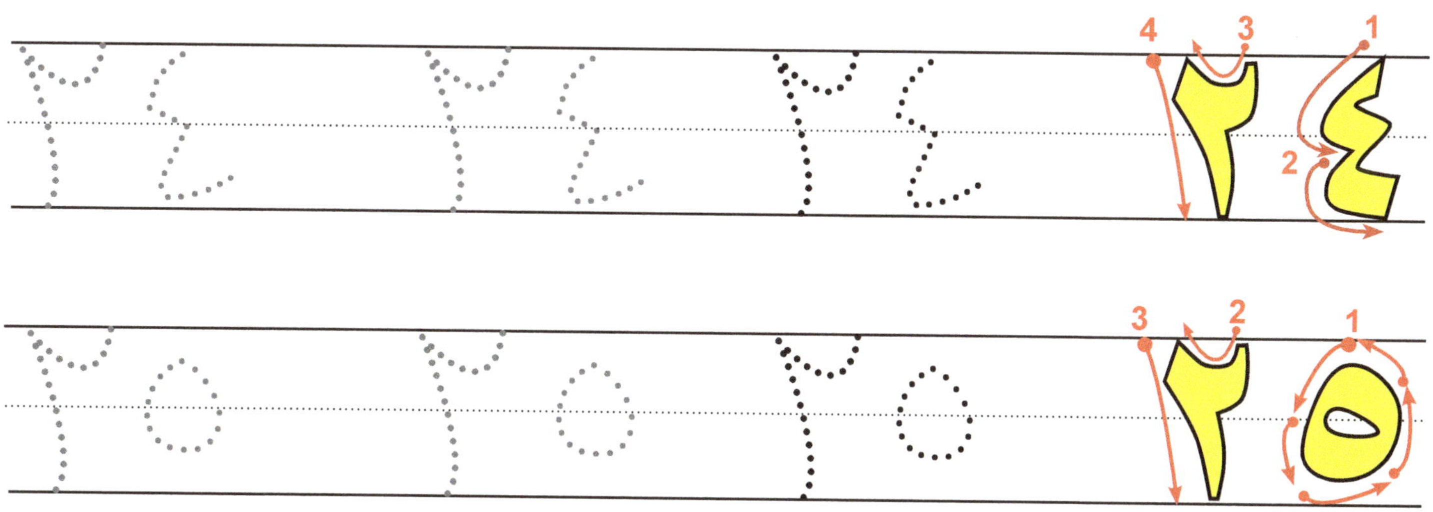

أ ب ت ث ج ح خ د ذ ر ز س ش ص ض ط ظ ع غ ف ق ك ل م ن هـ و ي

Lets write our homework !

Copy letter Tha ذ inside the dresses.

Beginning

Middle

End

Lets write our homework !

Copy the numbers.

٢٤

٢٥

Draw the shape muthallath then colour it aṣfar.

Lesson 15 : ر Ra

Head

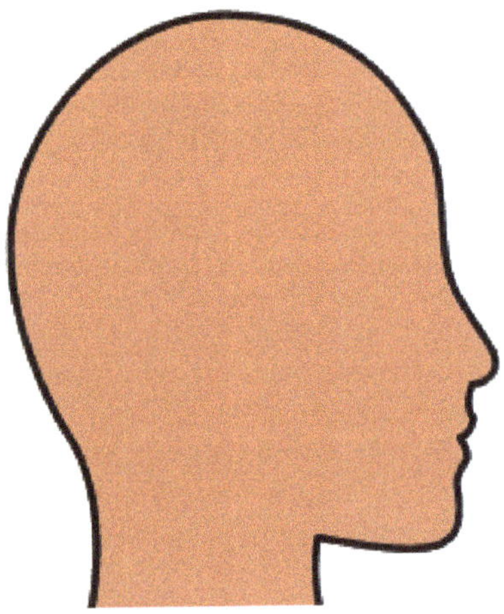

رَأْسْ Ra's

Remember

ر Is a light and an unfriendly letter!

أ ب ت ث ج ح خ د ذ ر ز س ش ص ض ط ظ ع غ ف ق ك ل م ن هـ و ي

Trace letter Ra ر خَطِّطْ الحَرْفْ

*Start writing from the right

1

Colour letter ر at the beginning of each word ahmar.

رَافِعَة  رَاكُونْ 

ر Is an unfriendly letter

Letter ر is an unfriendly letter, look how it only holds one hand from the back when joining in the middle of a word:

Now look how letter ر is not holding hands from the front when it comes at the beginning of a word:

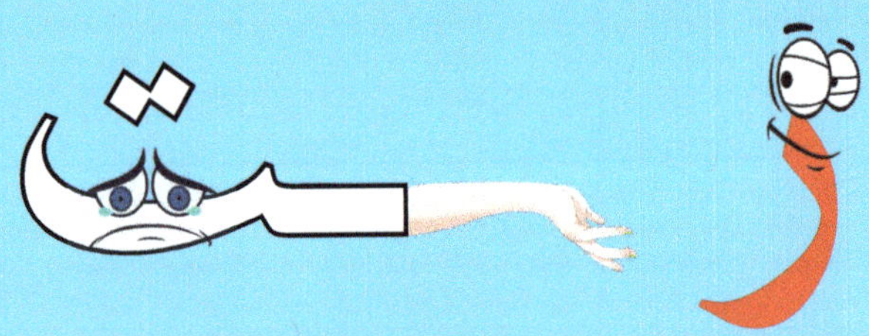

And finally, look how letter ر gives only one hand from the back when joining at the end of a word:

The shapes of Ra ر when joining

Letter Ra can change dresses when joining other letters at the:

End | Middle | Beginning

Colour letter Ra dresses :
at the beginning asfar, in the middle aswad and at the end banafsajy.

كُرْسِي   عَنْبَرْ   رَادْيُو

letter Ra ر with short vowels

With Fat-hah Ra

With Dammah Ru

With Sukoon/Silent R

With Kasrah Ri

Match letter Ra ر with its suitable hat or sock.

رَ رِ رُ رْ

Trace letter Ra with short vowels.

Match letter Ra with the correct word.

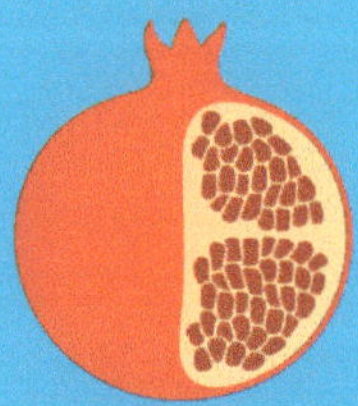

رُمَّانَة

Pomegranate Rummaanah

رِسَالَة

Letter Risaalah

رَمْلْ

Sand Raml

نَارْ

Fire Naar

ر

ر

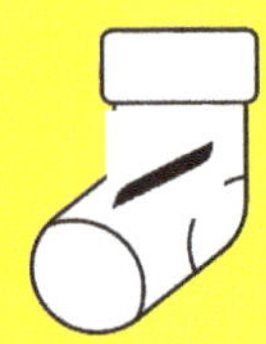

ر

ر

Trace letter Ra ر at the beginning, middle and end.

The Arabic numbers

Twenty six-Sittah wa īshroon

سِتَّة وَ عِشْرُونْ

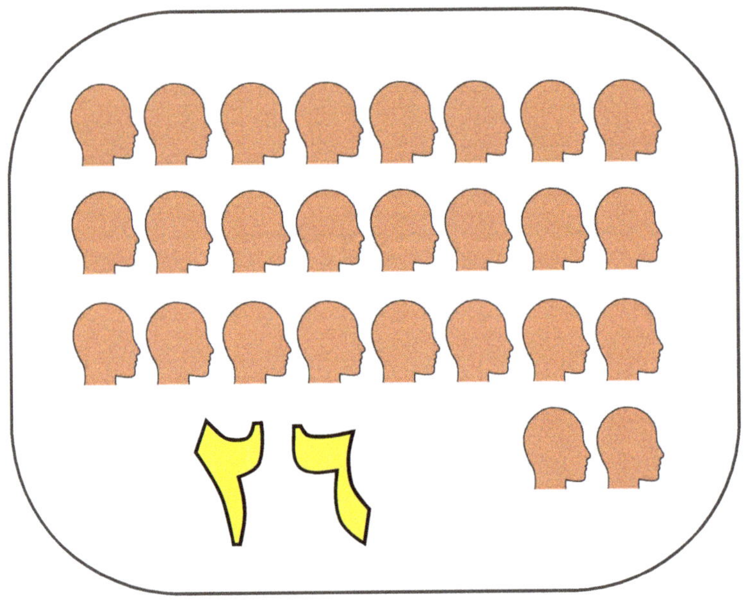

Twenty seven-Sabāah wa īshroon

سَبْعَة وَ عِشْرُونْ

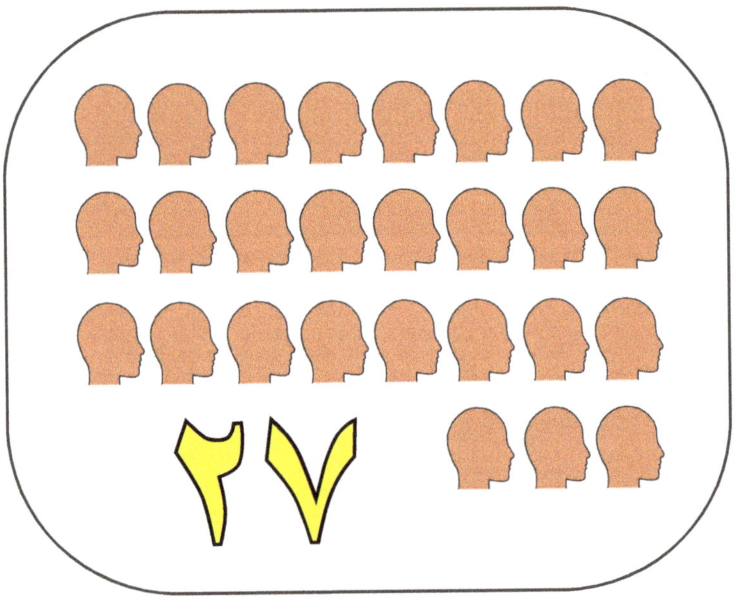

Trace.

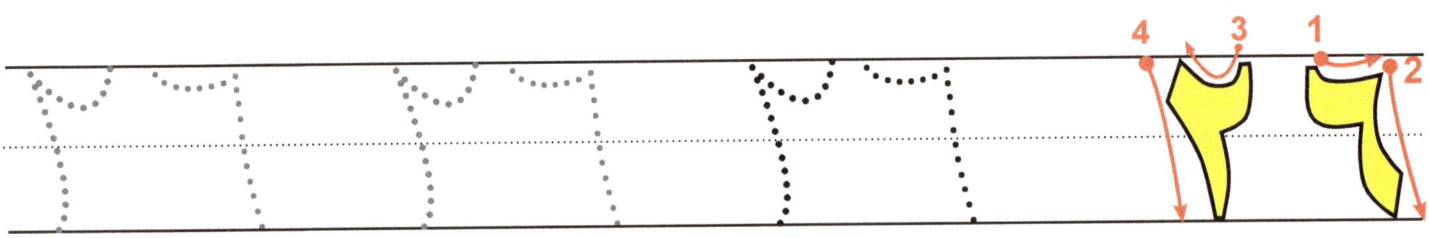

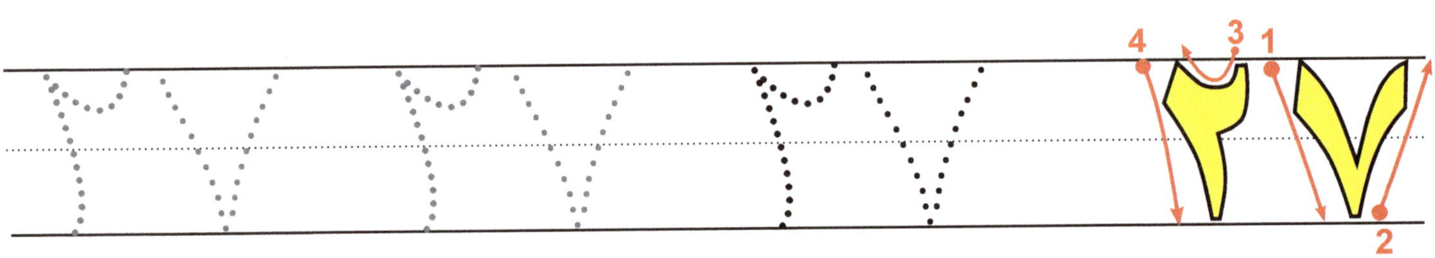

أ ب ت ث ج ح خ د ذ ر ز س ش ص ض ط ظ ع غ ف ق ك ل م ن هـ و ي

Lets write our homework !

Copy letter Ra ر inside the dresses.

Beginning

Middle

End

Lets write our homework !

Copy the numbers.

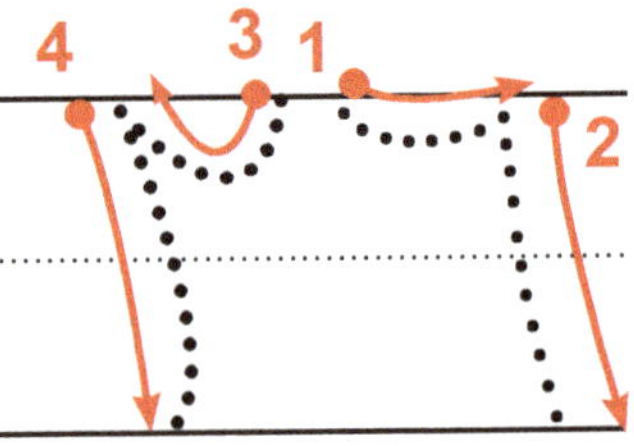

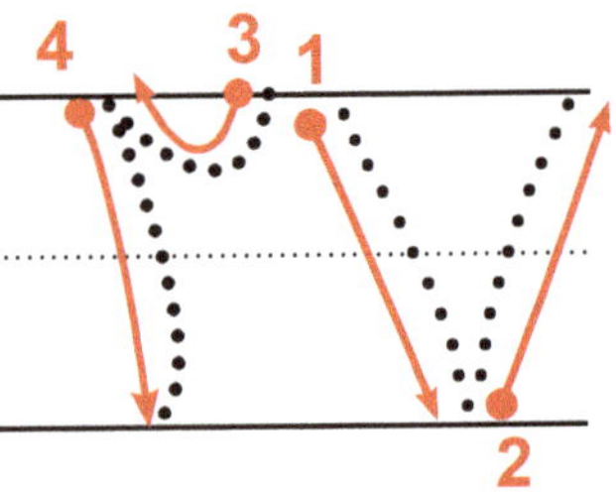

Draw the shape mustateel then colour it azraq.

Lesson 16 : ز Za

Giraffe

زَرَافَة Zaraafah

Remember

ز Is a light and an unfriendly letter!

Trace letter Za ز خَطِّطْ الحَرْفْ

*Start writing from the right

Colour letter ز at the beginning of each word **bonny.**

رَافِعَة 

رَاكُون 

ز Is an unfriendly letter

Letter ز is an unfriendly letter, look how it only holds one hand from the back when joining in the middle of a word:

Now look how letter ز is not holding hands from the front when it comes at the beginning of a word:

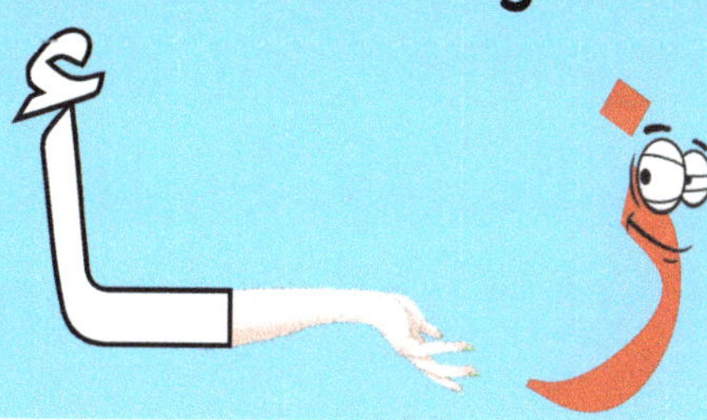

And finally, look how letter ز gives only one hand from the back when joining at the end of a word:

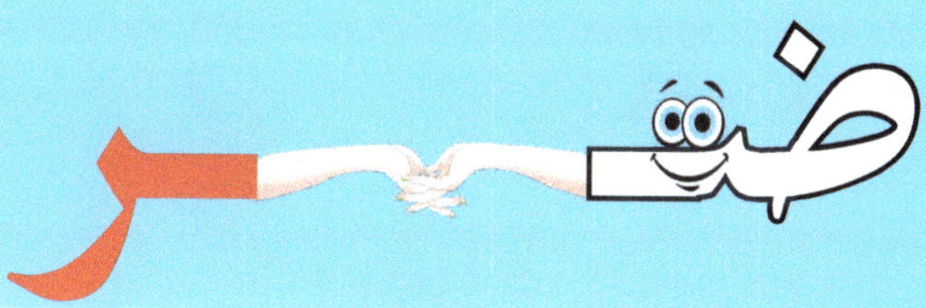

The shapes of Za ز when joining

Letter Za can change dresses when joining other letters at the:

End

Middle

Beginning

Colour letter Za dresses :
at the beginning bonny, in the middle abya<u>dh</u>
and at the end zahry.

جَزَرْ

زَهْرَة

لُغْزْ

With Fat-ḥah Za زَ

With Dammah Zu زُ

With Sukoon/Silent Z زْ

With Kasrah Zi زِ

Match letter Za زَ with its suitable hat or sock.

زْ زُ زَ زِ

Trace letter Za with short vowels.

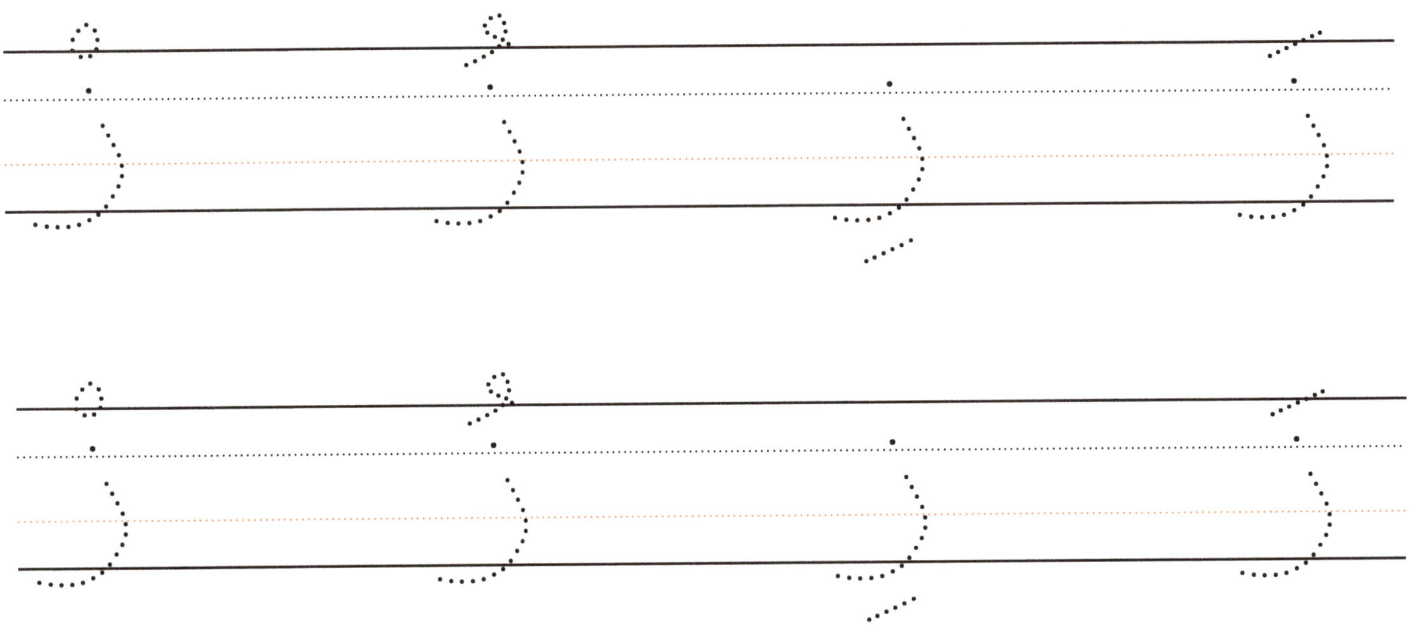

Match letter Za with the correct word.

زِينَة

Decoration Zeenah

زَوْرَق

Boat Zawraq

تِلْفَازْ

Television Tilfaaz

زُجَاجْ

Glass Zujaaj

ز

ز

ز

ز

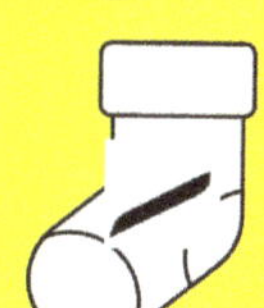

Trace letter Za ز at the beginning, middle and end.

The Arabic numbers

Twenty eight-Thamaaniyah wa ῑshroon

ثَمانِيَة وَ عِشْرُونْ

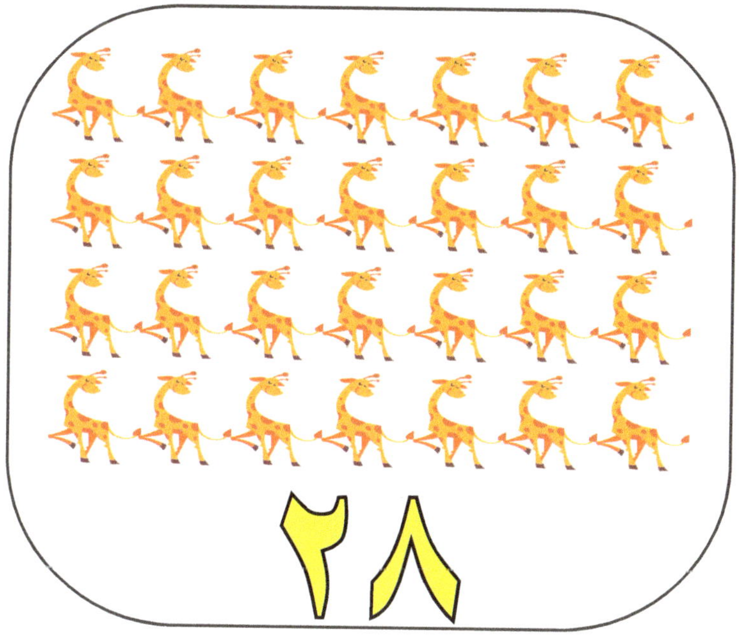

Twenty nine-Tisāah wa ῑshroon

تِسْعَة وَ عِشْرُونْ

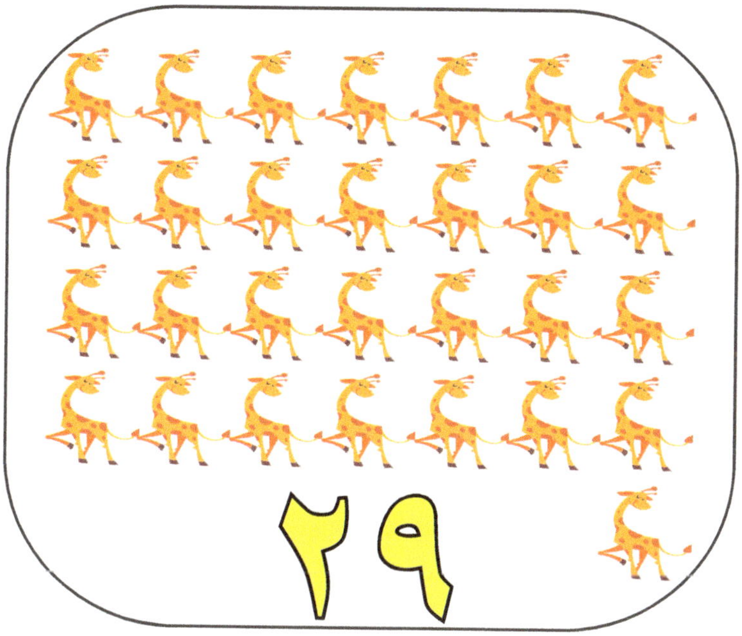

Trace.

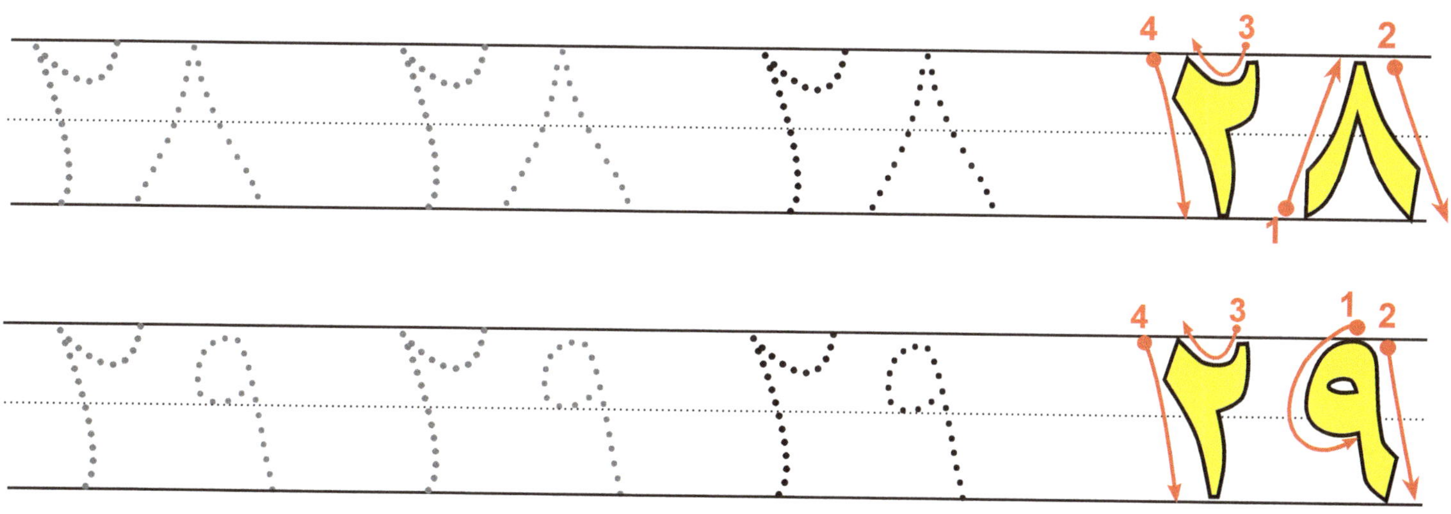

أ ب ت ث ج ح خ د ذ ر ز س ش ص ض ط ظ ع غ ف ق ك ل م ن هـ و ي

Lets write our homework !

Copy letter Za ز inside the dresses.

Lets write our homework !

Copy the numbers.

٢٨

٢٩

Draw the shape murabaā then colour it banafsajy.

Lesson 17: Revision - trace.

Alphabet revision

Colour all the letters you learned in this book.

Choose from the colours akhdar, banafsajy, ahmar, burtuqaaly, bonny, asfar, zahry and azraq.

أ ب ت ث ج ح خ

د ذ ر ز س ش ص

ض ط ظ ع غ ف ق

ك ل م ن هـ و ي

Numbers revision - trace.

١٤ ١٥ ١٦

١٧ ١٨ ١٩

٢٠ ٢١ ٢٢

٢٣ ٢٤ ٢٥

٢٦ ٢٧ ٢٨ ٢٩

Numbers revision

Colour all the numbers you learned in this book.

Choose from the colours akhdar, banafsajy, ahmar, burtuqaaly, bonny, asfar, zahry and azraq.

١٧	١٦	١٥	١٤
٢١	٢٠	١٩	١٨
٢٥	٢٤	٢٣	٢٢
٢٩	٢٨	٢٧	٢٦
٣٣	٣٢	٣١	٣٠

تم بحمد الله .

With Allah's grace, this workbook has been completed.

﴿ وَقُلْ رَبِّ زِدْنِي عِلْمًا ﴾ .

And say, My Lord, increase me in knowledge.